D0125424

Did you know that studying history can be fun?

BRING HISTORY TO LIFE by becoming a history investigator. Examine the evidence (primary and secondary source materials); cross-examine the people and witnesses. Take a look at what was happening at the time—but be careful! What happened years ago might suddenly become incredibly interesting and change the way you think!

Contents

Taking On History

A huge crowd gathered in Grant Park, in Chicago, Illinois, on election night, 2008.

Around 200,000 people crowded Grant Park in downtown Chicago, Illinois, on the night of November 4, 2008. It was the night of the presidential election. The crowd was waiting for news. They had gathered for a rally in support of Democratic **candidate** Barack Obama. Obama would later be making either a speech of victory or a speech of defeat. A large screen showing a news channel's coverage of the election kept the crowd up-to-date. One by one, each state was declared as belonging to either Obama or Republican candidate John McCain. T-shirts, buttons, paper signs, and huge, homemade banners were everywhere. They were covered with words such as *hope*, *change*, and simply *Obama*.

The excitement grew as the night progressed. Obama was in the lead. He would make history if he won. The United States has historically been led by white men. Obama was half African. He called himself a "skinny guy with a funny name." Could he win the presidency?

T-shirts and signs were some of the many ways people showed their support for Barack Obama during the election.

NIGHT RALLY IN PHOENIX, ARIZONA.

CHAPTER 1

BORN ON AN ISLAND

Because he lived in Kenya, Barack Obama Sr. did not play a major role in raising his son.

STANLEY ANN DUNHAM WAS born in Kansas in 1942. Her father had wanted a boy so badly that he named his daughter after himself. She went by her middle name. The small family moved around the country as Ann's father went from job to job. They finally settled in the state of Washington in 1955. The family moved to Hawaii after Ann finished high school in 1959. Ann became a student at the University of Hawaii. It was there that she met Barack Obama. Obama was a charming student from Kenya. He was attending the university on a **scholarship** from the Kenyan government. The couple was married in 1961. Ann gave birth to a baby boy soon after.

Obama had a happy childhood in Hawaii.

The Young Family

Barack Hussein Obama Jr. was born on August 4, 1961, in Honolulu, Hawaii. The name Barack means "blessed." Young Barack was born during a time of change in the United States. The fight for **civil rights** for African Americans was reaching its height. Martin Luther King Jr. had begun organizing peaceful protests and demonstrations less than six years before. Having an African father and a white American mother meant that Obama was born into the middle of the struggle.

The family was lucky in many ways. The American South was being torn apart by racial differences. Demonstrators and volunteers supporting civil rights were often beaten or killed. The marriage between Barack's parents was considered illegal in some parts of the nation. But Hawaii was more welcoming of diversity. People of many different races lived together on the small

Leading up to and during his presidency, some people questioned whether Barack Obama was born in the United States. He released his birth certificate in 2011 to prove that he was born a U.S. citizen in Hawaii. See page 60 for a link to view the birth certificate online.

island chain far off in the Pacific Ocean. The Obamas' marriage was unusual for the time. But it was not an impossibility.

Not long after Obama was born, Barack Sr. graduated from the University of Hawaii. He was offered a scholarship to Harvard University in Massachusetts to continue his studies. The scholarship paid for his classes and his own living expenses. But it would not be enough to support the whole family. The Obamas decided to separate for the time being. Barack Sr. left for Massachusetts. Ann stayed in Hawaii with their son and her parents.

Obama became interested in sports at a young age.

YESTERDAY'S HEADLINES

Major steps toward equal rights for African Americans took place during the 1950s and 1960s. Segregation, or the separation of people according to race, legally ended in public schools with the *Brown v. Board of Education* decision in 1954. The Freedom Rides took place during the summer of 1961. Young white and black college students organized to end segregation on interstate buses. They rode buses from Washington, D.C., south toward New Orleans, Louisiana. The buses were often stopped, and the students were beaten or arrested. The Freedom Riders were finally victorious in November, when segregation on interstate buses was ended. Barack Obama was just three months old.

Changes

Ann Obama depended on her parents to help raise her son. Stanley and Madelyn Dunham were known as Gramps and Toot to young Barry, as Barack was called. They would play a large role in his life in the years to come. Ann worked and completed her degree while Barry spent time with his grandparents. He played on the beach and heard stories about his father, his mother's childhood, and his grandparents' time living in Kansas.

Ann and Barack Sr. were divorced in 1964, and Barack Sr. returned to Kenya. Ann decided it was best to keep her family in Hawaii. Ann soon met a student named Lolo Soetoro at the university. Lolo was from Indonesia, an island chain in Southeast Asia. Lolo asked Ann to marry him in 1967, and she agreed. Lolo moved back to Indonesia immediately to put things in order for his new family. Ann planned to follow afterward with Barry. The months in between were filled with packing and other preparations.

Life in Indonesia

Ann and Barry soon arrived in the Indonesian capital city of Jakarta. Life was difficult at first. Barry and Ann had to learn a new language. Barry started attending a Catholic school named Franciscus Assisi Primary. He faced some trouble fitting in. He was the school's only foreign student. But he did manage to make some friends. The family's home was better than most in Indonesia. It was made of brick and cement and had a red tile roof.

Obama and his grandfather, Stanley, enjoyed visiting Hawaii's beaches.

Obama and his family lived in Indonesia during the late 1960s and early 1970s.

Barry lived face-to-face with serious poverty in Indonesia. Electricity was not available in many parts of the country. Even where it was available, most Indonesians could not afford it. Beggars filled the streets and sometimes came to the door. The government in Indonesia was corrupt. Many Indonesians were under a constant threat of being captured or forced out of the country by the army or police.

Lolo worked at first as a geologist for the Indonesian government. He soon worked his way up and was given a job with an American oil company. Ann found a job teaching English at the U.S. Embassy. The family grew wealthier and moved to a better house in a new neighborhood. The family also grew in size with the birth of Barry's little sister, Maya.

Barry left Franciscus Assisi to attend a public school instead. But Ann did not believe that the school provided a good enough education. She enrolled Barry in an American **correspondence** course so he could keep up with U.S. schools. She woke him every day at 4:00 a.m. to go through the lessons. She eventually decided that this was not enough. In 1971, she sent Barry back to Hawaii to live with his grandparents. He would complete his education there.

Obama went by the name Barry Soetoro during his time at Franciscus Assisi.

ANGKA NILAI

No. _203._

1. Nama murid : _Barry Soetoro_   L / P

2. Tempat dan tanggal lahir : _Honolulu_ _4-8-61_
3. Bangsa: a. Warga negara : _Indonesia_
   b. Keturunan asing :
   c. Suku bangsa :
4. Agama : _Islam_
5. Alamat murid : _Ment. Dalem R007/Rw03_
6. Dari sekolah mana (dipindahkan) dan kelas berapa: _Taman Hawah Strata Asisia_

7. a. Diterima disekolah ini tgl.: _1-1-1968_
   b. Ditempatkan dikelas : _I_

8. a. Nama orang tua Ajah / Ibu : _L. Soetoro m.a._

   b. Pekerdjaan : _Peg. Dinas Geografi Dit. Top. A.D._
   (nama ibu diisi, hanja djika ajah sudah meninggal)
   c. Alamat : _Ment. Balen R1007/Rw03_

9. a. Nama wali :
   (hanja diisi, djika orang tua murid tak ada, sudah meninggal atau karena hal lain)
   b. Pekerdjaan :
   c. Alamat :
10. Meninggalkan sekolah ini :

    A. Belum tamat. Keluar dari kelas _____ tanggal _____
       Kemana _____ Sebab _Pindah_
    B. Tamat, menerima idjazah tanggal _____
    C. Melandjutkan sekolah ke _____ No. _____

11. Keterangan lain :

15

Obama was a star player on his high school basketball team.

Back in Hawaii

Barry began fifth grade in the elite, private Punahou
School. Hawaii's wealthiest families sent their children
there. Barry was one of a handful of black students. But
he made a large and diverse group of friends. He played
basketball for the school. His skills on the court earned
him the nickname Barry O'Bomber.

His mother and sister joined him in Honolulu in 1972.
Ann returned to the University of Hawaii as a graduate

student. Barry's father made a brief visit to Hawaii during this time. Barack Sr. had been in a car crash in Kenya. He decided to spend part of his recovery with his American son. Barack Sr. returned to Kenya after about a month. It was the last time Barry saw his father, though the two of them exchanged letters occasionally until Barack Sr.'s death years later.

In 1975, Ann decided to move back to Indonesia as part of her studies. She gave Barry a choice. He could either join her and Maya or remain in Honolulu. He chose to stay. Barry spent the rest of his high school days at Punahou

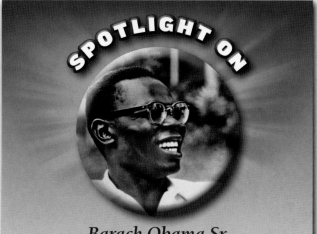

SPOTLIGHT ON

Barack Obama Sr.

Barack Obama Sr. was born in Alego, Kenya, in 1936. He was the son of Hussein Onyango Obama, an important member of the small village. Barack grew up herding his father's goats before being offered the chance to study in the city of Nairobi. When he was 23, he was sent to the University of Hawaii to study economics on a scholarship from the Kenyan government. Kenya offered these scholarships to its brightest students in hopes that they would bring what they learned back to Kenya and help modernize the country. Obama did just that after earning his doctorate from Harvard. He worked in the Kenyan government as an economist. He only returned to the United States once, in the early 1970s, to see his son Barack.

and lived with his grandparents. He graduated in 1979 and set his sights on college.

CHAPTER 2

ORGANIZING CHICAGO

Obama's time at Occidental College helped him develop the public speaking skills he would later use to succeed in politics.

IN COLLEGE, OBAMA GOT HIS first taste of the public spotlight. His first two years were spent at Occidental College, or "Oxy," in Los Angeles, California. He became involved in a student organization working to create awareness of racial segregation in South Africa. He opened a rally with a short speech and a bit of acting. While he was talking, two white peers wearing black suits and sunglasses walked up behind him and dragged him away. The event was meant to highlight the lack of freedoms that people had under the South African government. It also gave Obama an experience in public speaking that he would never forget.

Living in New York City was a new experience for Obama.

New Place, New Name

Obama made the most of his time at Oxy. But he
decided he needed a change after two years there. He
transferred to Columbia University in New York City
in 1981. He began going by Barack instead of the more
casual Barry. He began to take his work more seriously.
He spent much more of his time studying.

Obama later remembered his time in New York as
one of discovery. He remembered the poverty he had
seen in Indonesia. He had also often witnessed violent

anger from African American and other **minority** groups in Los Angeles as a student at Oxy. These experiences came together in New York as he compared the living conditions, education systems, and job opportunities of black, Hispanic, Arab, and other minority Americans to those of the white population. He decided the system had to change.

By the time he graduated in 1983, he had decided to become a community organizer. He would create change in society and the government by working with everyday people and communities. But he received no responses when he sent out letters asking organizations and politicians about jobs.

Poor New York City neighborhoods opened Obama's eyes to the potential for social change.

He took a job instead as a research assistant with a consulting firm that provided business advice to major companies. He was soon promoted to being a writer of financial news. Despite his success, Obama was not satisfied with his job.

Finding His Way

Obama quit his job as a financial writer after about a year. Weeks later, he was given an interview with a civil rights organization. The interview went so well that he was offered a job on the spot. Obama's education and background would allow him to represent black communities in meetings with corporations and government leaders. But he refused the position.

Obama's move to Chicago set him on the path to becoming president.

He wanted to be a **grassroots** organizer on the streets instead of spending his time in offices and meetings.

It was months before Obama found what he was looking for. He continued to send out letters to civil rights organizations and politicians. He finally received a call for a job interview from Mike Kruglik with the Developing Communities Project (DCP) and Calumet Community Religious Conference (CCRC).

The DCP worked in communities on the South Side of Chicago, Illinois. The CCRC focused on the nearby suburbs. Both organizations worked to improve job opportunities after the recent decline of Chicago's steel industry. Factories were closing,

YESTERDAY'S HEADLINES

Chicago's steel industry began in the mid-19th century. Steel mills sprang up around the area. Many of them were located in the city's South Side, in Calumet and Joliet to the south, and in northeastern Indiana. The United States produced more than half of the world's steel at the beginning of the 20th century. The Chicago area produced about 20 percent of that. The steel industry suddenly collapsed during the 1970s and 1980s. Steel could be produced more cheaply in other countries. American mills could not keep up. Many Chicago steel mills closed. About 16,000 people lost their jobs between 1979 and 1986.

Angry workers tried to fight the companies that put them out of work, but there was little they could do.

and the companies were sending their jobs elsewhere. As a result, the communities that had depended on factory jobs were suffering. Kruglik focused the two organizations' efforts at local churches. He believed that churches were where most people found their sense of community. Involving churches was the best way to reach the most people.

DCP leaders asked Obama to help them run the organization in the city. Obama would be working on the street and talking with people in the communities.

After some thought, he accepted. He was given enough money to buy a car, drive to Chicago, and get himself set up in the city. He left New York one week after the meeting. The year was 1985.

Chicago

Chicago was the city of Harold Washington in 1985. Washington had been elected Chicago's first African American mayor two years before. African American and other minority communities felt the city was changing. Obama saw pictures of the mayor in businesses, homes, and offices. But Chicago was still one of the most segregated cities in the country.

Obama spent most of his time working in the Roseland neighborhood and a **public housing project** called Altgeld Gardens. He began by talking to members of the communities. He interviewed 20 to 30 people

SPOTLIGHT ON

Harold Washington

Harold Washington was born in 1922 in Chicago, Illinois. After serving in World War II (1939–1945), he went to college and in 1952 earned his law degree. He practiced law for a short time before entering politics. He ran for mayor of Chicago in 1983 and won, becoming the first African American mayor in the city's history. With the support of several new city council members, he easily won a second term in 1987. He died of a heart attack not long after the election, before he had a chance to make any real changes to the city.

A FIRSTHAND LOOK AT
ASBESTOS AND ALTGELD GARDENS

Asbestos is a dangerous substance that was once used in the construction of buildings. It is now known to cause cancer and other health problems. Asbestos was found in the Altgeld Gardens housing project in 1986. The DCP helped organize meetings with government officials to find and remove the asbestos. See page 60 for a link to a newspaper article covering the issue.

every week. He worked out of an office in a church on Chicago's West Side. Progress was slow at first.

Obama began accomplishing larger victories with the DCP less than a year after arriving in Chicago. He helped open an office that assisted people to find jobs in the area. The opening was an opportunity

Obama's work helped make Altgeld Gardens a safer place for the people who live there today.

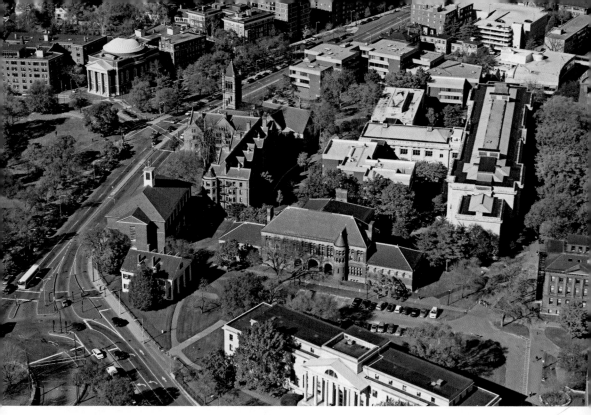

Harvard is one of the most respected law schools in the country.

for celebration. Even Mayor Washington made an appearance. The DCP helped the Park District work on cleaning up neighborhood parks. It also helped organize neighborhood watch programs in several areas to cut down on crime. More and more people were joining the organization.

Obama spent the next few years organizing residents to help improve their community. But he decided after three years that he needed a change. He could make a difference organizing just as he did with the DCP. But he could also make a difference by working in law. Obama began applying to law schools. He decided on Harvard, the same school his father had attended. He set off to Massachusetts in 1988.

CHAPTER 3

THE BEGINNING OF POLITICS

Obama quickly found success as a law student.

OBAMA DID WELL AT HARVARD

Law School. His grades were good enough for him to become involved in the *Harvard Law Review*. The highly respected journal publishes articles on law written by students, professors, and practicing lawyers. Obama's peers eventually encouraged him to run for editor, an important position on the journal. He succeeded at the age of 28, becoming the journal's first African American editor. His success was largely because of his ability to see all sides of an issue. Those who voted for him believed he would work hard to represent everyone equally, whether he agreed with them or not. This ability would serve him well years later as he entered the world of politics.

Meeting Michelle

One summer during his time in law school, Obama returned to Chicago. He spent the break as a summer associate with a law firm in the city. The firm assigned him an adviser named Michelle Robinson. Michelle was a graduate of Harvard Law School herself. She was smart, confident, and pretty. Obama decided he wanted to know her better. He asked her out on a date.

Obama married Michelle soon after graduating from law school.

At first she said no. She argued that it was a bad idea. First of all, she was his adviser. And second, she and Obama were the only two African Americans working at the law firm at the time. She worried that their coworkers would think the relationship was too predictable. She tried introducing him to other women in the hopes that he would fall for someone else.

But Obama kept asking her out. Michelle eventually agreed. He later wrote that they went for ice cream.

The date was a success. The two remained together through the rest of Obama's time at Harvard. Obama graduated from Harvard Law with honors in 1991. He and Michelle were married on October 3, 1992.

Back in Chicago

The Obamas settled down in Hyde Park in southern Chicago. Barack went back to organizing for a time. He also started practicing law as a civil rights lawyer. He represented people whose rights had been ignored or compromised in some way. He also taught classes at the University of Chicago as a law professor.

In 1994, **scandal** forced Congressman Mel Reynolds of Illinois to leave office. There would be a new election to determine who would take his place. Illinois state senator Alice Palmer decided to try for Reynolds's old

The University of Chicago was a perfect fit for Obama's legal talents.

TODAY'S PERSPECTIVE

Obama received some attention in the newspapers when he became editor of the *Harvard Law Review*. Publishers contacted him to ask if he wanted to write a book. He accepted. After years of writing and rewriting, his memoir *Dreams from My Father* was published in 1995. Obama wrote about growing up, community organizing, and visiting his father's family in Kenya. The book was not very successful when it was first published. But Obama's name became better known as his political career gained steam. The book was rereleased in 2004. This time it was a best seller.

seat. Someone would have to take her spot in the Illinois Senate if she won the race for the U.S. Congress. She announced that Barack Obama would be the perfect candidate.

Running for State Senate

The election would take place in 1996. But the **campaign** started long before then. Obama ran as a member of the Democratic Party, the same political party Palmer belonged to. The first step was to gather signatures. A candidate needed at least 757 signatures from **registered** voters to be included on the election ballot. Election ballots list the candidates running for a political office. Obama went door-to-door and held rallies around southern Chicago. He was able to gather plenty of signatures by the deadline.

But in the middle of his efforts, he learned that Palmer had lost in her run for U.S. Congress. Palmer now turned her attention to winning her old seat in the Illinois Senate. Obama suddenly found himself facing unexpected competition.

Because she had entered the race late, Palmer had only weeks to gather the required signatures to get her name on the ballot. She ended up submitting more than 1,000 names. Her success made Obama and his campaign team suspicious. After double-checking the signatures, they decided to take Palmer to court and challenge some of the signatures. While they were doing

Obama set his sights on the state capitol in Springfield, Illinois.

Malia is the Obamas' elder daughter.

this, they challenged the signatures of the other two Democratic candidates. All three candidates were kicked out of the race. None of them had enough acceptable signatures to be included on the ballot.

Obama had cleared the way to the state senate election. Chicagoans typically voted for Democrats. Obama's Republican opponent had little chance of winning. Obama won the election in 1996. In 1997, he took his seat as an Illinois state senator.

Victories and Losses

Obama spent the next eight years in the Illinois Senate. His family grew during this time. Malia Obama was born in 1998. The Obamas welcomed a second daughter three years later. They named her Natasha. Her name was quickly shortened to Sasha.

As a senator, Obama established a name for himself as a supporter of **ethics** laws. He also became known as a persuasive speaker. Republicans and Democrats alike found themselves changing their minds after hearing him speak.

Obama's time in the state senate was not always easy. He occasionally faced jealousy or lack of support from fellow Democrats. He was a favorite of the senate's

Malia (right) and Sasha (left) often join their father at political events.

Democratic leader, Emil Jones. Jones sometimes gave Obama responsibilities such as presenting new bills or being a spokesman for important issues. These jobs usually were given to more experienced senators.

Obama decided in 2000 that it was time to run for a seat in the U.S. House of Representatives. His main opponent was Bobby Rush. Rush had already served four terms in the office and was better known than Obama. He won the race easily. Obama stayed in the Illinois Senate.

Obama learned important political skills during his time in the state senate.

Bobby Rush's (center) popularity helped him to defeat Obama easily in the U.S. House of Representatives election in 2000.

Bigger Opportunities

Another opportunity arose four years after losing the race against Rush. A seat opened up in the U.S. Senate. Obama entered the race. He used the slogan "Yes, We Can." He had better luck this time. Two other Democrats had also decided to run for the office. But both lost support in the middle of their campaigns after suffering major scandals. Obama found himself with a clear path to the ballot. The Republicans chose Alan Keyes as their candidate. Keyes was a well-known but not well-supported politician. He had a tendency to say the wrong thing and anger voters.

SPOTLIGHT ON

Getting into the U.S. Senate

Senators rarely leave their positions once they are elected the first time. The longest-serving senator served more than 50 years. It is common for a senator to serve for decades. This means there is rarely an open seat.

It is even harder for an African American to find a seat. There have been six African American senators in U.S. history. Only three have served in the last 130 years. There were no African American U.S. senators in 2011. In comparison, the House of Representatives has had 132 African American members. More than 40 had seats in 2011.

Obama won 70 percent of the vote, one of the largest percentages in Illinois history. He became the third African American in the U.S. Senate since 1877.

Obama was given the chance of a lifetime during his campaign for the U.S. Senate. The presidential elections were taking place the same year, 2004. In each election the political parties announce their candidates for president and vice president at huge conventions. A keynote speaker is chosen to give a speech on an important theme. That year, Barack Obama was chosen as the keynote speaker for the Democratic Convention.

The speech he gave would prove historic. Obama chose to talk about the problems of party politics. He believed that there was too much competition between the major political parties. He thought they should try

The 2004 Democratic National Convention thrust Obama into the national spotlight.

harder to work together. He spoke about the need for the country to unify in order to improve. The speech brought Obama's name and face to the United States.

A FIRSTHAND LOOK AT
OBAMA'S KEYNOTE ADDRESS

Barack Obama's speech at the 2004 Democratic National Convention made him a household name. It introduced him to a national audience. It also sped him on his way to the presidency. See page 60 for a link to read the speech online.

CHAPTER 4

THE PRESIDENCY

Obama's win in the 2004 Senate race was a major milestone in his political career.

OBAMA'S KEYNOTE ADDRESS AT the Democratic National Convention opened doors for him. He and his advisers had a meeting. With the popularity Obama gained with his speech, he could possibly run for president. At first, they discussed running in 2012 or 2016. But these plans soon changed. Obama's popularity never faded as he entered his first year in the U.S. Senate in 2005. He was a new senator and had little power. But he was in the news almost constantly. The public was excited about him. Obama and his advisers believed this was their opportunity. He announced on a cold day in February 2007 that he would run for president in the 2008 election.

Hillary Clinton was Obama's main competition in the primaries.

The Primaries

Obama had to win in the **primaries** first. This series of elections determines who will run as the party's candidate. Each state provides a certain number of **delegates** to the winner. The number of delegates is based on the number of voters in the state. Most people assumed that Hillary Clinton would win in the Democratic primaries. She was well known as a U.S. senator and former First Lady. But Obama was determined to win the Democratic **nomination**.

Obama and his team ran the campaign using grassroots methods similar to the ones he had used years before in Chicago. They created a Web site where supporters could donate money. The site also let supporters register local Obama campaign groups. This allowed groups of volunteers to run small, local campaigns. There was also a blog to keep supporters up-to-date and videos documenting the campaign.

Obama went from town to town. He spoke to individuals and ran rallies that attracted thousands of supporters. In a surprise victory, he won the Iowa **caucus**. Clinton came in third. She won the next two states before Obama won again in South Carolina.

The two continued going back and forth. Clinton often won primaries in states that had more delegates. Obama won in a large number of smaller states. He pulled far ahead of Clinton as the primaries progressed into the spring of 2008. The competition continued

Hillary Clinton became one of Obama's biggest supporters during the presidential race.

until Clinton decided in June to drop out of the race and support Obama's campaign. He accepted the Democratic Party's nomination on August 28.

Obama knew that many people considered him an inexperienced politician. To help counter these arguments, he chose experienced U.S. senator Joe Biden as his running mate. Biden had been a member of the U.S. Senate since 1973. He would become vice president if Obama won.

The Race Is On

The Republicans chose Senator John McCain as their presidential candidate. Alaska governor Sarah Palin was his running mate.

John McCain (at microphone) was Obama's main opponent in the 2008 election.

Obama's strong speaking skills and positive message helped him gain supporters all around the country.

Obama based his campaign on the ideas of "Hope" and "Change." These words often appeared on the posters, T-shirts, buttons, and other merchandise sold to supporters. His slogan began as "Change We Can Believe In." It was later changed to "Change We Need." He often repeated the phrase he had used in his U.S. Senate campaign, "Yes, We Can." This focus, along with his Web site and grassroots techniques, made him appealing to young people and minority communities. His efforts highlighted his relative youth in a positive light. He was 47 years old at the time. McCain was 72.

McCain used Obama's youth and inexperience against him. McCain had been in the Senate for decades, with a solid political career and experience in the military.

A VIEW FROM ABR★AD

Obama went on a trip to countries around the world during the 2008 presidential campaign. The visits served as a kind of test run for his presidency. Obama did not have much experience in international politics. He had to prove to voters he could work with other countries. Some Americans didn't like this. They thought Obama was acting as if he were president even though the race was not over. Many people in the countries he visited felt differently. He spoke to a crowd of thousands in Germany. The crowd reacted to his speech with cheers, and the German media spoke positively of the visit.

Obama had served less than one term in the U.S. Senate and had never served in the military. One of the main issues the candidates dealt with was the ongoing conflicts in Afghanistan and Iraq. Both wars were costing lives and money. McCain's military experience gave some voters confidence in his ability to make the right decisions regarding those countries.

A crisis just weeks before the election had a major effect on voter opinion. The American economy collapsed in September 2008. Stock prices fell, and many people lost a lot of money. McCain reacted by temporarily halting his campaign. In spite of a planned public debate against Obama, McCain took a plane to Washington, D.C., to attend to pressing Senate business. The debate had to wait. Obama insisted that the presidential candidates

The enormous crowd at Grant Park cheered as Obama's victory was announced.

had little power and could do nothing to help until one of them was elected. He also seized the chance to blame the current Republican-run government for the economic problems.

Obama was the clear winner when the election finally took place on November 4. He claimed about 53 percent of the vote. He made history by being the first African American to win the presidency. On January 20, 2009, Barack Obama was inaugurated.

The Challenges of Change

The new president hit the ground running. He began by working to create closer relationships with foreign nations. Many Americans were worried that the previous president, George W. Bush, had damaged relations with other countries. They were especially concerned about countries in the Middle East. Bush had ordered the invasions of Afghanistan and Iraq. These invasions overthrew both nations' governments. He had also supported policies that often targeted Arabs, Arab Americans, and Muslims following the September 11 attacks in 2001.

Obama focused his energy on the Middle East in the early days of his presidency.

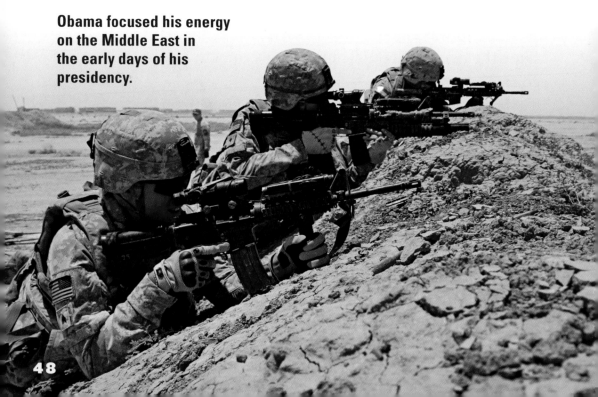

Obama first demanded the closing of the infamous U.S. prison in Guantánamo Bay, Cuba. The prison had suffered a series of scandals years before. The public had learned of severe interrogation techniques military officials used on suspected terrorists. Obama also visited Cairo, Egypt, to show support for the Muslim world. These actions and the promise of similar actions to come resulted in Obama winning the Nobel Peace Prize in 2009.

Obama's popularity faltered as his presidency continued. The United States was not recovering from the September 2008 economic collapse as quickly as many people

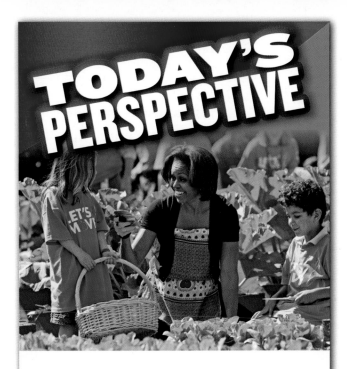

TODAY'S PERSPECTIVE

Michelle Obama was very involved in her husband's campaign. She is also outspoken about her own views. Her frequent speeches in 2008 made her a recognizable voice of the Obama campaign. Some of her comments earned her critics. But she is also beloved by many. She has made the covers of *Newsweek* and *Ebony* magazines.

Following in the footsteps of many great first ladies, Michelle Obama has taken an active role in many causes. Her causes include supporting military families and improving nutrition for young people. She also planted the White House's first vegetable garden since the one planted by First Lady Eleanor Roosevelt during World War II.

had hoped. Also, despite his demands, the Guantánamo Bay detention center was still open.

Obama had long promised reform in national health care. Many voters had been excited about this issue during the presidential election. But the issue lost support when a new health care bill came under debate in Congress. The bill passed in Congress in March 2010 after months of debate. Obama signed it into law on March 23. The bill brought health care to 30 million people. But it also created new taxes, mostly for the wealthy. Some people considered the law unconstitutional because it gave the government too much power.

Obama faced a major disaster in 2010. The Deepwater Horizon oil rig exploded and leaked millions of barrels of oil into the ocean. The accident caused serious damage to the environment. The leak took

The Deepwater Horizon spill was one of the first major events Obama had to deal with in his presidency.

Obama announced the death of Osama bin Laden in a special television broadcast.

months to close off. The disaster caused a serious drop in the president's popularity.

Meanwhile, the wars in Afghanistan and Iraq continued. Obama had been promising to pull American troops out of the countries since his campaign in 2008. He was able to start bringing soldiers home from Iraq in 2010. But thousands of troops remained overseas. His efforts to end U.S. combat in Iraq were made easier in 2011. Obama announced on May 1 that U.S. forces had captured and killed terrorist Osama bin Laden. Bin Laden had been behind the attacks on September 11, 2001. He had been on the run ever since. The capture was a huge victory for the Obama administration. Thousands more troops in both Iraq and Afghanistan were able to come home as the year progressed.

What Happened Where?

UNITED STATES

Chicago

Washington, D.C.

Honolulu

ATLANTIC OCEAN

Honolulu, Hawaii Obama was born in Honolulu, Hawaii, on August 4, 1961. He spent much of his childhood there.

Chicago, Illinois Obama first arrived in Chicago to organize communities on the city's South Side. He later represented sections of Chicago in the Illinois Senate. He also held his presidential election rally in Chicago's Grant Park.

PACIFIC OCEAN

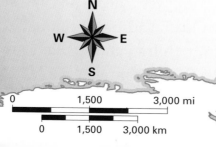

N
W   E
S

0	1,500	3,000 mi
0	1,500	3,000 km

ARCTIC OCEAN

Nairobi, Kenya Barack Obama Sr. was born in Kenya. He went to school in Nairobi and later lived there while working for the Kenyan government.

Jakarta, Indonesia Obama and his mother moved to Jakarta after she married Lolo Soetoro in 1967. Obama lived there until 1971.

KENYA
Nairobi

Jakarta
INDONESIA

*INDIAN
OCEAN*

Back on the
★ Campaign Trail

Obama has established strong relationships with world leaders such as Russian president Dmitri Medvedev.

As of 2012, Barack Obama's first term as president is not yet over. He is involved in ongoing talks with Russian leaders. U.S. involvement in Afghanistan and Iraq continues, even as troops are returning home. Relationships between the United States and several North African and Middle Eastern countries have become rocky. Revolutions in Libya, Tunisia, Egypt, and

IN 2012, ELECTION DAY WILL

other countries threaten to shake the region apart.

Obama's first term as president officially ends in January 2013. But presidents are allowed to serve two terms. On April 4, 2011, Obama announced that he would run for reelection in 2012.

Obama's presidency has already made history whether he wins again or not. He is the first African American president. He has inspired many people who are part of minority communities to dream of new possibilities. Obama has seen economic failures and recovery during his time as president. He has worked on new policies during a major oil spill and the cleanup that followed. He has brought thousands of troops home from Afghanistan and Iraq, and he oversaw the capture and death of Osama bin Laden. With these successes and failures behind him, Barack Obama again brings the promise of hope and change to a new presidential campaign.

Obama's legacy as president will be determined in future years.

TAKE PLACE ON NOVEMBER 6.

NFLUENTIAL INDIVIDUALS

Harold Washington (1922–1987) was elected mayor of Chicago, Illinois, in 1983. He served as the city's first African American mayor during the years Obama worked as a community organizer in Chicago.

Madelyn Dunham (1922–2008) was Obama's grandmother. In a time when few women held jobs, she worked her way up from secretary to vice president of a bank. She died two days before the 2008 presidential election.

Barack Obama Sr.

Lolo Soetoro (1935–1987) was a student at the University of Hawaii when he met Ann Dunham. The two married, and he, Ann, and Barack moved to Indonesia. Lolo and Ann were divorced in 1980.

Barack Obama Sr. (1936–1982) was Barack Jr.'s father. He was born in a village in Kenya and studied in the United States. Though absent most of his son's life, he had a significant effect on Barack Jr.'s thoughts and actions growing up.

John McCain (1936–) was the Republican candidate during the 2008 presidential race.

Stanley Ann Dunham Soetoro (1942–1995) was Barack Obama's mother. She married and divorced twice, once to Barack Obama Sr. and once to Lolo Soetoro. She earned her doctorate in anthropology from the University of Hawaii. She spent most of her adult life living and working in Indonesia.

Stanley Ann Dunham Soetoro

Joe Biden (1942–) was Obama's running mate in the 2008 presidential election. He became vice president in 2009. His experience as a senator helped Obama's presidential campaign.

Michelle Obama (1964–) is Barack Obama's wife and the First Lady. She graduated from Princeton University and attended Harvard Law School. She met Barack while working as his adviser at a Chicago law firm.

Malia Obama (1998–) is Barack and Michelle's elder daughter.

Natasha "Sasha" Obama (2001–) is Barack and Michelle's younger daughter.

Michelle Obama

TIMELINE

1961

February
Barack Obama and Ann Dunham are married.

August 4
Barack Hussein Obama Jr. is born.

1964

Barack Obama Sr. and Ann Dunham are divorced; Barack Sr. returns to Kenya.

1967

Ann Dunham and Lolo Soetoro are married; Barack and Ann move to Indonesia.

1985

Obama moves to Chicago to work as an organizer.

1988

Obama starts law school at Harvard University in Massachusetts.

1992

October 3
Barack Obama and Michelle Robinson are married.

2001

Sasha Obama is born.

2004

Obama delivers the keynote address at the Democratic National Convention; he is elected to the U.S. Senate.

1971
Barack returns to Hawaii to study at Punahou School.

1979
Obama graduates from high school; he begins attending Occidental College in California.

1981
Obama transfers to Columbia University in New York.

1997
Obama begins his first term in the Illinois Senate.

1998
Malia Obama is born.

2000
Obama runs for a seat in the U.S. House of Representatives. He loses to Bobby Rush.

2008
August 28
Obama accepts the Democratic nomination for president.

November 4
Obama wins the presidential election.

2009
January 20
Obama is sworn into office, becoming the first African American president in history.

LIVING HISTORY

Primary sources provide firsthand evidence about a topic. Witnesses to a historical event create primary sources. They include autobiographies, newspaper reports of the time, oral histories, photographs, and memoirs. A secondary source analyzes primary sources, and is one step or more removed from the event. Secondary sources include textbooks, encyclopedias, and commentaries.

Asbestos and Altgeld Gardens In 1986, Barack Obama and the DCP helped raise awareness about the presence of asbestos in Altgeld Gardens. Several local newspapers covered the story. To view one of the articles from the *Chicago Tribune*, visit *http://articles .chicagotribune.com/1986-05-29/news/8602080537_1_cha-asbestos -residents*

Barack Obama's Birth Certificate Some people doubted that Obama had been born in the United States. In 2011, Obama released an official birth certificate, proving that he was a native-born U.S. citizen. To view the document, visit *www.whitehouse.gov /blog/2011/04/27/president-obamas-long-form-birth-certificate*

Obama's Keynote Address Obama was asked to deliver the keynote speech at the Democratic Convention in 2004. The speech introduced him to the American public and launched his national political career. To watch a video and read the speech online, visit *www.americanrhetoric.com/speeches/convention2004 /barackobama2004dnc.htm*

President Barack Obama's Inaugural Address Barack Obama's first speech as president was made at his inauguration ceremony. To watch a video of the speech, visit *www.whitehouse .gov/blog/inaugural-address*

Books

Abramson, Jill. *Obama: The Historic Journey*. New York: Callaway, 2009.

Colbert, David. *Michelle Obama: An American Story*. Boston: Houghton Mifflin, 2009.

Edwards, Roberta. *Who Is Barack Obama?* New York: Grosset & Dunlap, 2010.

Falk, Laine. *Meet President Barack Obama*. New York: Children's Press, 2009.

Katirgis, Jane. *Celebrating the Obama Family in Pictures*. Berkeley Heights, NJ: Enslow Publishers, 2010.

President Obama: A Day in the Life of America's Leader. New York: Time for Kids Books, 2009.

Thomas, Garen Eileen. *Yes We Can: A Biography of President Barack Obama*. New York: Feiwel and Friends, 2008.

Tieck, Sarah. *Sasha & Malia Obama*. Edina, MN: ABDO Publishing, 2010.

Web Sites

CNN Election Center 2008—Barack Obama
www.cnn.com/ELECTION/2008/candidates/barack.obama.html
Read stories, look at pictures, and watch videos of Obama's speeches during the historic 2008 presidential election.

The White House—President Barack Obama
www.whitehouse.gov
Learn about what is going on at the White House and stay up-to-date on major events in Obama's presidency.

**Visit this Scholastic Web site for more information on Barack Obama:
www.factsfornow.scholastic.com**

GLOSSARY

campaign (kam-PAYN) a series of actions organized over a period of time in order to achieve or win something, as in an election

candidate (KAN-dih-date) a person who applies for a job or runs for public office

caucus (CAW-kus) a meeting where political party members choose which candidates to nominate for office

civil rights (SIV-uhl RITES) the rights belonging to a nation's citizens

correspondence (kor-es-PON-denss) written communication

delegates (DEH-luh-guts) people who represent a larger group of people at a meeting

ethics (EH-thiks) a set of principles or moral values

grassroots (GRAS-roots) an organizing technique that focuses on everyday people to create change

minority (muh-NOR-i-tee) a group of people of a particular race, ethnic group, or religion living among a larger group of a different race, ethnic group, or religion

nomination (nah-mih-NAY-shuhn) the official appointment of a candidate

primaries (PRY-mer-eez) a series of elections to determine the presidential candidates

public housing project (PUH-blik HOWZ-ing PRAH-ject) a form of housing provided by the government to people who cannot afford homes

registered (REJ-uh-sturd) entered one's name on an official list

scandal (SKAN-duhl) an event that causes public outrage because it involves unethical or illegal actions

scholarship (SKAH-lur-ship) a form of financial support granted to students

INDEX

Page numbers in *italics* indicate illustrations.

ABOUT THE AUTHOR

Jennifer Zeiger earned her bachelor's degree from DePaul University. She now lives in Chicago, Illinois, editing and writing books for children. She spent the 2008 presidential election volunteering on the South Side of Chicago, encouraging people to vote.